YOUR KNOWLEDGE HAS VALUE

AF145744

- We will publish your bachelor's and master's thesis, essays and papers

- Your own eBook and book - sold worldwide in all relevant shops

- Earn money with each sale

Upload your text at www.GRIN.com
and publish for free

GRIN

Bibliographic information published by the German National Library:

The German National Library lists this publication in the National Bibliography; detailed bibliographic data are available on the Internet at http://dnb.dnb.de .

Imprint:

Copyright © 2017 GRIN Verlag, Open Publishing GmbH
Print and binding: Books on Demand GmbH, Norderstedt Germany
ISBN: 9783668537507

This book at GRIN:

http://www.grin.com/en/e-book/376005/strategic-international-management-international-strategic-approaches

Anonym

Strategic International Management. International Strategic Approaches, Transnational Strategy, and Joint Ventures in China

GRIN Publishing

GRIN - Your knowledge has value

Since its foundation in 1998, GRIN has specialized in publishing academic texts by students, college teachers and other academics as e-book and printed book. The website www.grin.com is an ideal platform for presenting term papers, final papers, scientific essays, dissertations and specialist books.

Visit us on the internet:

http://www.grin.com/

http://www.facebook.com/grincom

http://www.twitter.com/grin_com

Strategic International Management

Assignment

Table of contents

List of Abbreviations

Cf.	Confer (compare)
CJV	Contractual Joint Venture
e.g.	Exempli gratia (for example)
EJV	Equity Joint Venture
GDP	Gross Domestic Product
HQ	headquarter
IJV	International Joint Venture
IR	Integration-Responsiveness
JV	Joint Venture
LTD	Limited
MNE	Multinational Enterprise
MS	Microsoft
R&D	Research and Development
U.S.	United States
WTO	World Trade Organization

List of Tables

List of Figures

1. International Strategies

1.1 Introduction

Multinational companies[1] face a fundamental strategic dilemma when competing internationally: the global-local dilemma. On one hand, there are pressures to respond to the unique needs of the markets per country or region. On the other, there are efficiency pressures that encourage companies to deemphasize local differences and to conduct business similarly throughout the world.[2] The orientation of an organization or the individual industrial sector can already determine a certain strategy. Some industries are already internationally oriented, whilst others are rather domestic.[3] *Bartlett* and *Ghoshal* developed a framework with four basic strategic approaches which companies can integrate to respond to forces for global integration, local responsiveness, or both.[4] Within this chapter, a theoretical understanding for these strategies should be formed. To deliver a practical example, *Microsoft* will be analyzed for its strategic approach based on publicly available information. It is necessary to say that the framework is ideal and very few companies fit precisely into any one category.[5] There have also been several interpretations of these strategies from other authors, but as the *Bartlett/Ghoshal* typology is most commonly used and has been very influential in literature it will form the basis for the further explanations.[6] The *Integrative-Responsiveness-Grid* will be explained in chapter two of this assignment.

1.2 International Strategy (or Home Replication Strategy)

Companies implement an international strategy when they leverage core competencies from their parent country around the globe. Thus, the international strategy emphasizes replicating home-country-based competencies which requires foreign units to operate activities that are configured and coordinated by

---

[1] Within the further explanations the term *Multinational Enterprise* or *Multinational Company* will be used to describe a firm which outside its home-country. That does not necessarily mean it is applying a *Multinational Strategy*.
[2] Cf. Cullen and Parboteeah (2014, p. 216)
[3] Cf. Radebaugh, Daniels, and Sullivan (2014, pp. 503–509); Deresky (2016, pp. 312–313)
[4] Cf. Bartlett and Beamish (2013); Bartlett and Ghoshal (2002)
[5] Cf. Mead and Andrews (2009, p. 315)
[6] Cf. Morschett, Schramm-Klein, and Zentes (2015, p. 33); Kutschker and Schmid (2011, pp. 297–298)

the HQ. The basic assumption is that the organizational structure of the parent company is superior to those of the subsidiaries, thus it should be replicated abroad. Ultimate control resides with executives within the home-country, given their reasoning that they best understand the company's core competencies. Testing of new ideas will be fulfilled in the home market. Goods and services will first be introduced in the domestic market and at a later stage into foreign markets. Especially companies with a strong brand name and high reputation can succeed with this strategy. It transfers core competencies to units in foreign markets where rivals lack a competitive alternative. It works well when industry conditions do not demand high degrees of global integration or local responsiveness, and the company's business practices set market standards, or most of the firm's customers are in its home market. Unaltered expansion of these competitive advantages to foreign markets incurs moderate operational costs, yet earns high profits. The approach is particularly straightforward and usually the first strategy adopted, when firms venture abroad. However, the headquarters' one-way view from the home-country to the rest of the world may misread opportunities and threats in foreign markets. Centralizing a company's value chain within the home country often weakens configuration efficiency and coordination flexibility. An international strategy might safe costs in the first steps of a company's internationalization process but potentially leads to misinterpret local circumstances in foreign markets. An unexpectedly enterprising competitor may disrupt the foreign industry structure and take over a market.[7]

1.3 Multinational Strategy (or Localization Strategy)

The assumption that cultural differences are best factored in if the enterprise relies on market-specific expertise and an extended presence in the diverse countries forms the basis of the multinational strategy. Companies that face high pressure for local responsiveness and low need for global integration tend to apply this strategy. Usually unique local cultural, legal-political, and/or economic conditions spur the MNE to adapt its value activities. Basically, the firm's value-chain design follows the lead of foreign operations instead of the headquarters'.

---

[7] Cf. Radebaugh et al. (2014, pp. 509–511); Peng and Meyer (2016, pp. 423–424); Bartlett and Beamish (2013, p. 113); de Kluyver (2010, pp. 213–217); Trompenaars and Hampden-Turner (2012, pp. 229–230)

The company differentiates products to respond to foreign differences. Local affiliates are considered as competent domestic actors in their respective country. They enjoy a high degree of freedom with respect to their actions and are given a large amount of autonomy. A reduced need for central support to manage local activities as well as a greater sensitivity for local preferences are key advantages of this approach. Localizing the value chain also reduces risks of damaging the company's local reputation or losing money due to increased exchange-rates. While the MNE's affiliates adopt the value-chain to local preferences, they still can take advantage of the parent's global operations - local competitors lack of this support. The multinational strategy results in management, design, production, and marketing activities within each subsidiary and therefore raises costs. The MNE basically operates "mini-me" units around the world. Different product designs require different materials, smaller markets make for shorter production runs, different channel structures call for dissimilar distribution formats, and divergent technology platforms complicate information exchange. As allocating authority to local decision makers can create powerful subsidiaries, which may on any given configuration or coordination matter opt not to follow headquarters' policy and instead maintaining that their situation warrants a different approach. HQ must resort to persuasion instead of command. The difficulty of this task escalates as the number of subsidiaries rises. All of this makes the multinational strategy impractical in cost-sensitive situations and requires many resources for coordination capabilities.[8]

1.4 Global Strategy (or Global Standards Strategy)

By applying a global strategy, the same product with little variation (if any) is offered on different markets, without consideration of regional differences in customer habits. The main difference to an international strategy is that the global strategy views the world as a single marketplace. In contrast, a company applying an international strategy would mainly target customer needs of its home market. Hence, the global approach targets universal needs or wants that support selling standardized products worldwide and emphasizes volume, cost minimization, and efficiency. It assumes that consumer preferences in different countries are

---

[8] Cf. Radebaugh et al. (2014, pp. 510–512); Peng and Meyer (2016, pp. 424–425); Bartlett and Beamish (2013, p. 113); de Kluyver (2010, pp. 213–217)

highly similar, if not identical. If there are differences, consumers will sacrifice them to buy a high-quality, low-priced substitute. Researchers state that the integration of global markets, e.g. institutional developments to reduce trade frictions and investment restrictions, further promotes this development. Ultimately, consumers' disposition to discount nationalism girds the global strategy. Usually industries with high demand for global integration and low pressure for local responsiveness adapt the global approach. It strictly centralizes transactions of the enterprise and its subsidiaries, country-specific conditions are excluded from consideration. Efficiency standards push the MNE to achieve cost leadership in its industry, if not, it must be competitive with the industry's pacesetter. This requires to aggressively exploit location economies to maximize scale effects. Using resources for anything other than improving efficiency would negatively affect competitiveness. The supreme advantage of this strategy is leveraging economies of scale. Configuring and coordinating activities to capture scale effects drives the global efficiencies needed to compete with like-minded rivals and to convince consumers to forsake national preference for global products. Single-minded focus on improving efficiency also clarifies decision-making: if any ambiguity occurs within the strategic analysis, global integration trumps local differentiation - always. However, using a single approach for a global market is operationally risky: Change of all sorts is an intrinsic feature of international business. A disruptive innovation turns the single-minded focus of a globally tuned value chain into a maladapted delusion. The global strategy reduces learning opportunities by given the dominance of a global standard. It also requires increased coordination to regulate a global matrix of inputs and outputs.[9]

1.5 Transnational Strategy

Especially MNEs that force a high pressure for both, local responsiveness and global integration need to configure a different type of value chain. These companies need to deal with an environment of interconnected consumers, industries, and markets. They must exploit location economies while also applying coordination methods that leverage core competencies, and reconcile a

---

[9] Cf. Radebaugh et al. (2014, pp. 510–513); Peng and Meyer (2016, pp. 424–426); Bartlett and Beamish (2013, p. 113); de Kluyver (2010, pp. 213–217)

complex mix of global and local pressures. Managing this feat enables the MNE to implement a transnational strategy, thereby differentiation capabilities and contributions per country, finding ways to learn systematically from various environments, and diffusing this knowledge throughout its global operations. Basically, this means the transnational strategy combines multinational and global approaches: It takes the regional specifics into consideration, tries to use global efficiency by limiting the variations of a product, and introduces it unaltered in various markets whenever possible. Thus, it simultaneously manages the tensions of global integration and local differentiation in ways that leverage specialized knowledge and promote worldwide learning. The underlying managerial approach and the degree to which power is transferred to the subsidiaries are not standardized. Rather than top-down or bottom-up coordination, the transnational strategy promotes knowledge flows from idea generators to idea adopters, no matter where one or the other resides. Headquarters applies systems to motivate communication and collaboration. The strategy is flexible and may be altered according to the needs with the purpose to reach maximum efficiency. In summary, it supports efficiency, compels effectiveness, and leverages learning that drive innovations to serve global and local markets. Vitality of learning enables managers to respond to changing environments, reorienting activities without imposing additional bureaucracy. Ultimately, these capabilities support standardizing activities to generate global efficiencies without overly discounting the demands of responsiveness. A transnational strategy encourages sophisticated coordination methods to diffuse the lessons learned at one unit to other business units. On the other hand, it requires elaborate mechanisms to integrate dispersed operations. It is difficult to specify in theory and complex to implement in practice. Limitations arise from complicated agendas, high costs, and cognitive limits. Thus, it's tough to configure, coordinate, and prone to performance shortfalls. Reconciling IR-pressures, further complicated by the mission to upgrade knowledge worldwide, can overwhelm the best-intentioned MNEs. Developing a network mindset among employees, installing the requisite communication network, and navigating the ambiguity of multi-criteria decision making is expensive. Such costs are especially burdensome when slowing economies call for streamlining activities.[10] Following table summarizes the differences between the four strategic approaches.

	International Strategy	Multinational Strategy	Global Strategy	Transnational Strategy
Strategic orientation	Leverage core competencies and home country innovations into competitive positions abroad.	Building flexibility to respond to national differences through strong, resourceful, and entrepreneurial national operations	Building cost advantages through centralized global-scale operations	Developing global efficiency, flexibility, and worldwide learning capability simultaneously
Value Chain Configuration	Concentrated, value activities are set and directed by the home office	Dispersed; subsidiaries command discretion to adapt value activities to local conditions.	Concentrated; value chain configuration exploits location economics.	Concentrated to tap location economies. Dispersed, subject to minimum efficiency standards, to meet local preferences.
Value Chain Coordination	Centralized coordination processes as parent retains control of value activities to apply, regulate, and protect core competencies.	Subsidiaries operate quasi-independently. Autonomy lets them adapt activity to local marketplace circumstances.	Industry pressures to maximize standardization and contain costs require coordinating value activities operations from a global perspective.	Simultaneous goal of integration and responsiveness calls for sharing coordination between headquarters or subsidiaries.
IR Grid Positioning	Low pressure for global integration, low pressure for local responsiveness	Low pressure for global integration, high pressure for national responsiveness.	High pressure for global integration. Low pressur for local responsiveness.	High pressure for global integration, high pressure for local responsiveness.
Role of Subsidiaries	Sale of HQ products	Identification and exploitation of local opportunities	Implementation of HQ strategies	Differentiated contribution to the worldwide competitive advantages of the MNC
Network Model	Centralized hub	Decentralized federation	Centralized Hub	Integrated network
Vertical Product Flows	High, sequential	Low	High, sequential	Bidirectional
Inter subsidiary product flows	Low	Low	Low	High

---

[10] Cf. Radebaugh et al. (2014, pp. 509–514); Peng and Meyer (2016, pp. 424–426); de Kluyver (2010, pp. 213–217) de Kluyver (2010, pp. 213–217)

	International Strategy	Multinational Strategy	Global Strategy	Transnational Strategy
Central-ization of Decisions	High	Low	High	Medium (decentralized centralization)
Manage-ment Transfers, Visits, Joint Working Teams	Low	Low	High	High
Centers of Excellence	Low	Low	Low	High
Product Mod-ification	Low	High	Low	High
Local Pro-duction	Low	High	Low	Medium
Depen-dency	Strong dependence	In-dependence	Strong dependence	Inter-dependence
Advantages	- Leverages home country-based advantages - Relatively easy to implement	- Maximizes local responsiveness	- Leverages low-cost advantages	- Cost efficient while being locally responsive - Engages in global learning and diffusion of innovations
Dis-advantages	- Lack of local responsiveness - May result in foreign customer alienation - Weak configuration efficiency and coordination flexibility	- High costs due to duplication of efforts in multiple countries - Too much local autonomy	- Lack of local responsiveness - Too much centralized control	- Organizationally complex - Difficult to implement
Examples	Kraft, Google, P&G, Nucor, Harley Davidson, Baidu, Apple, Carrefour	Unilever, Nestle, Heinz, The Body Shop, Mc Donald's, Johnson & Johnson, Pfizer, Embraer, Ranbaxy	Toyota, Canon, Haier, Texas Instruments, Caterpillar, Cemex, Infosys, Walmart, Huawei, Haier, LVMH, American Express, Nokia, Cisco	GE, Tata, Zara, IBM

Table 1: Characteristics of International Strategy Types[11]

---

[11] Adopted from Bartlett and Beamish (2013, pp. 198–201); Peng (2016, p. 406); Radebaugh et al. (2014, p. 510); Morschett et al. (2015, p. 35); Macharzina (1993, p. 83); Harzing (2000)

1.6 Microsoft's Strategy

Founded in 1975, *Microsoft* operates worldwide with offices in more than 100 countries. As its current vision, the company states: *"Microsoft is a technology company whose mission is to empower every person and every organization on the planet to achieve more. Our strategy is to build best-in-class platforms and productivity services for a mobile-first, cloud-first world."*[12] This part gathers the relevant publicly available information about the company to see if a strategic approach can be determined.

In 2013, *Microsoft*, in a reversal of its divisional structure, disbanded its eight product divisions and created four new ones arranged around broader functional themes to streamline its technologies and compete better with *Apple* and *Google* in the global mobile and internet markets. The goal was to reduce duplication and create more cooperative teamwork among the new managers.[13] *"The earlier approach, intended to copy the success of companies such as General Electric, had left Microsoft ill-prepared for the fast-moving technology world,"*[14] said Rob Helm, an analyst at Directions on *Microsoft*. Researchers state that *Microsoft's* corporate structure reflects the needs of the IT hardware and software business in response to market dynamics, which can be interpreted as a high need for global integration.[15]

The bulk of *Microsoft's* product development work takes place in Redmond, Washington, where the company is headquartered. The company also operates R&D facilities in other parts of the U.S. and around the world, including Canada, China, Denmark, Finland, France, India, Ireland, Israel, Japan, and the United Kingdom. The work of these foreign facilities is mainly limited to producing foreign language versions of popular *Microsoft* programs such as *Office*.[16] Microsoft itself states that it localizes many of its products to reflect local languages and conventions. This may require modifying the user interface, altering dialog boxes, and translating text.[17] However, in practice, the products are highly standardized for the global market: a person in any part of the world can start a program, even

---

[12] Microsoft Corporation (2016)
[13] Cf. Deresky (2016, p. 313); Wingfield (2013)
[14] Waters (2013)
[15] Cf. Lombardo (2017); Microsoft Corporation (2016)
[16] Cf. Jones and Hill (2012, p. 160); Microsoft Corporation (2016)
[17] Cf. Microsoft Corporation (2016)

without knowing the language.[18] This allows the company to garner significant scale economies, e.g. by spreading the $5 billion it cost to develop *Windows Vista* over global demand.[19]

One of the ways in which *Microsoft* can reach global markets and utilize these as an outlet to lower technology and information systems costs is through the strategy of outsourcing. In April of 2010 *Microsoft* signed a deal with an Indian outsourcer *Infosys Technologies LTD* to manage parts of the worldwide internal IT operations to cut IT costs.[20] Microsoft operates manufacturing facilities for the production and customization of phones, predominantly in Vietnam. The company announced the sale of its entry-level feature phone business in May 2016, which included the sale of its phone manufacturing facility. Other devices, as the famous *Surface Book*, are primarily manufactured by third-party contract manufacturers.[21] These manufacturing plants are located all over the world ensuring proximity to suppliers at the same time reducing transportation costs and negative environmental impact. The company generally can use other manufacturers if a current vendor becomes unavailable or unable to meet its requirements. Unlike many other corporations of similar size, *Microsoft* does not provide detailed data about the numbers and other details of its manufacturing plants around the globe. Cost advantage through outsourcing can be specified as the main source of value in *Microsoft's* operations.[22]

Summarizing these explanations, it becomes clear that *Microsoft* must follow a global strategic approach: The company is developing a product portfolio made for the global market without any intensive adaption of specific regional preferences. The failure of the Xbox gaming console in Japan might speaks for a lack of local responsiveness.[23] However, it can also be argued, that *Microsoft's* products achieved a versatility which doesn't require any local adaption beyond basic language. Furthermore, *Microsoft's* global sourcing underlines the conclusion of a global strategy, as companies using an international strategy

---

[18] Cf. Galvin, Hubbard, and Rice (2015, p. 321)
[19] Cf. Jones and Hill (2012, p. 149)
[20] Cf. Virginia's Community Colleges (2017); Microsoft Corporation (2016)
[21] Cf. Microsoft Corporation (2016)
[22] Cf. Dudovskiy (2017)
[23] Cf. McManus, White, and Botten (2008, p. 79); Ireland, Hoskisson, and Hitt (2006, pp. 170–171)

would mainly produce inland. However, it must be mentioned again, that very few companies fit precisely in one of these strategic categories. *Microsoft* in fact has made some local adaption of its products, e.g. adapting the Bing search engine to conform Chinese law by partnering up with hudong.com.[24] One might as well argue that the company runs a transnational approach or at least is on the transformation to it, if more insights about how the company handles innovation and learning processes, or regional responsiveness would be available.

---

[24] Cf. PR Newswire (2012)

2. Transnational Strategy – Environmental Requirements and Implementation Challenges

By applying a transnational strategy, companies attempt to coordinate and integrate operations across national boundaries to achieve potential synergies on a global scale. Management views the world as a series of interrelated markets. It has been mentioned, that the transnational approach is applicable within industries that force a high pressure for local responsiveness and global integration. This part will describe these environmental forces in detail, to allow a better understanding of how to determine the optimum conditions for applying this strategy. Furthermore, it will describe major challenges for its implementation.[25]

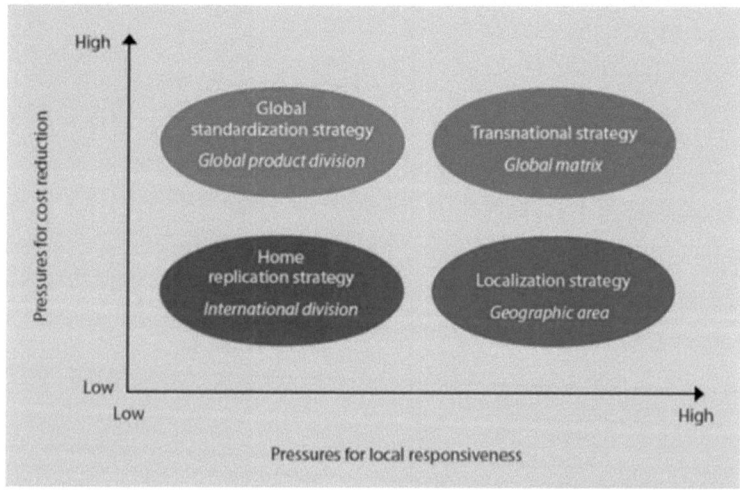

Figure 1: Multinational strategies and structures: The integration-responsiveness framework[26]

2.1 Local Differentiation vs. Global Integration

Companies that compete in the global marketplace typically face two types of competitive forces: pressures for global integration (or cost reductions) and pressures to be locally responsive. These competitive pressures place conflicting

---

[25] Cf. Hollensen (2016, pp. 428–429); Peng and Meyer (2016, 423-426);
[26] Source: Peng and Meyer (2016, p. 424)

demands on a company. *Figure 1* shows the so-called IR-Grid, which determines the right strategic choice depending on the degree of environmental pressures.[27]

2.1.1 Forces for Global Integration

Responding to pressures for global integration requires a firm to try to lower the costs of value creation. The forces for global integration, also called industry globalization drivers, can be divided into four categories:[28]

- **Market drivers:** Homogeneous customer needs in different markets may create opportunities to sell standardized products. Thereby marketing becomes transferable across countries. More and more often, companies also meet global customers, that are potentially purchasing. Additionally, global sales or e-commerce channels emerge in certain industries. These aspects enhance the need for globalization in an industry.

- **Cost drivers:** From a cost perspective, different industries have different incentives to standardize. Economies of scale, scope- and experience curves differ from industry to industry which can be caused by distinct production technologies. The greater the potential economies of scale and the steeper the experience curve, the more likely an industry is to turn global. Industries where product development is expensive and at the same time product lifecycles are short or technology is fast-changing usually try to use global scale effects. While global sourcing efficiencies might be given in an industry leading to concentration of supply and manufacturing, inter-country differences in labor costs and factor endowments might make concentration of production useful. Over the last few decades, logistics costs have generally been decreasing, making globalization easier to achieve. However, how energy prices, climate change, and technological innovations will influence logistics and consequently location strategies remain to be seen.

- **Governmental drivers**: Many governmental drivers also have an influence on the need for globalization in an industry. For example, uniform technical standards are necessary for product standardization, liberal trading regulations with low tariff and non-tariff barriers to trade, and common market regulations

---

[27] Jones and Hill (2012, pp. 153–154)
[28] Cf. Jones and Hill (2012, pp. 153–154); Bartlett and Beamish (2013, pp. 102–105); Morschett et al. (2015, pp. 29–31); Kutschker and Schmid (2011, pp. 299–306)

are drivers for globalization, making cross-border trade easier. Inversely, high trade barriers obviously reduce the forces towards globalization, protecting local particularities.

- **Competitive drivers:** As the most important driver, global competitors enhance the need for globalization. Only companies that manage their worldwide operations as interdependent units can implement and use a competitive strategy responding to threats in one market by reactions in others. Additionally, large MNEs offering the same products and brands around the world also promote the convergence of tastes and customer demands. International networks enhance the interdependence of countries and markets emerge in the presence of many MNEs.

The overall level of globalization of an industry can be measured by the ratio of cross-border trade to total worldwide production, the ratio of cross-border investment to total capital investment, the percentage of sales of worldwide standardized products, or the proportion of industry revenue generated by large MNEs.[29] Many commentators have argued that the liberalization of the world trade and investment environment in recent decades by facilitating greater international competition has generally increased cost pressures.[30]

2.1.2 Forces for Local Responsiveness

Pressures for local responsiveness arise from differences in consumer tastes, infrastructure, traditional practices, distribution channels, and host government demands. Responding to these kinds of pressures requires a company to differentiate its products, services, and marketing strategy from country to country to accommodate these factors, all of which tends to raise a company's cost structure.[31]

- **Differences in consumer tastes and preferences:** Strong pressures for local responsiveness emerge when customer tastes and preferences differ significantly between countries as they may for historic or cultural reasons. In such cases, a MNE's products, services, and marketing message must be customized to appeal to the tastes and preferences of local customers.

---

[29] Cf. Morschett et al. (2015, p. 31)
[30] Cf. Jones and Hill (2012, pp. 153–154);
[31] Cf. Jones and Hill (2012, pp. 154–155); Bartlett and Beamish (2013, pp. 106–112); Kutschker and Schmid (2011, pp. 299–306); Morschett et al. (2015, pp. 31–32)

- **Differences in infrastructure and traditional practices:** Pressures also arise from differences in infrastructure or traditional practices among countries, creating a need to customize products accordingly. Fulfilling this need may require the delegation of manufacturing and production functions to foreign subsidiaries.
- **Differences in distribution channels:** A company's marketing strategies may have to be responsive to differences in distribution channels among countries, which may necessitate the delegation of marketing functions to national subsidiaries.
- **Differences in host government demands:** Economic and political demands imposed by host country governments may require local responsiveness. More generally, threats of protectionism, economic nationalism, and local content rules (which require that a certain percentage of a product should be manufactured locally) dictate that international businesses manufacture locally.

Responding to pressures for cost reductions requires that a company tries to minimize its unit costs. To attain this goal, it may have to base its productive activities at the most favorable low-cost location, wherever in the world that might be. It also may have to offer a standardized product to the global marketplace to realize the cost savings that come from economies of scale and learning effects. On the other hand, responding to pressures to be locally responsive requires that a company differentiates its product offering and marketing per country or region to accommodate the diverse demands arising from national differences in consumer tastes and preferences, business practices, distribution channels, competitive conditions, and government policies. Because differentiation across countries can involve significant duplication and a lack of product standardization it may raise costs.[32] The global company assumes that the best-cost position is the key source of competitiveness; the multinational company sees differentiation as the primary way to enhance performance; and the international company expects to use innovations to reduce costs, enhance revenues or both. Companies adopting the transnational strategy recognize that each of this tradition approaches are partial. They need to deal with these contradictory forces simultaneously. Industries that simultaneously demand global efficiency and

---

[32] Cf. Jones and Hill (2012, pp. 153–154)

national responsiveness can also be called transnational industries. A company that indicates its business is influenced by these two forces simultaneously, might have the best conditions to justify the efforts for implementing a transnational strategy.[33]

2.2 The Case of *ITT*

Researchers *Bartlett* and *Ghoshal* mention the Case of *ITT,* a Puerto Rican telephone company, as an example on which a transnational strategy could have ensured the companies competitive advantage. By 1980, *ITT* was the second-largest supplier of telecommunications equipment in the world.[34] Under the influence of *ITT* founder and president, *Colonel Sosthenes Behn*, subsidiaries around the world strove to be local entities rather than parts of a global enterprise. All but the smallest national subsidiaries were set up as fully integrated, self-sufficient units, responsible for the development, manufacture, marketing, installation, and service of their products. Basically, *ITT* was following a multinational approach: The powerful, independent, and entrepreneurial national companies became the source of almost all major innovations. But the products that resulted varied considerably across worldwide operations because the local units insisted on tailoring systems to local technological needs. The company failed to integrate diverse product development efforts to standardize on a single global design. System houses would not give up the right to design and develop their own products, nor would they set aside traditional competitive rivalries and pool their capabilities or rely on the developments created in other national units. While this fragmentation led to some diseconomies, the company reaped political rewards for its ability to present a locally designed product to each national government. However, in the late 1970s, two simultaneous developments challenged the strategic posture of *ITT*: First, with the emergence of digital switching technology. Millions of dollars were needed to develop and build a new switch - no one country unit could manage such a large investment. Second, a trend toward deregulation opened many national markets to global competitors, thereby reducing the rewards of local differentiation. As a result, integrating the technological capabilities of the national entities to design a standard global

---

[33] Cf. Bartlett and Beamish (2013, pp. 200–201)
[34] Cf. ITT (2017)

product became a strategic imperative. *ITT* is a clear example on which external requirements, particularly cost and governmental drivers, require a multinational organization with the single focus on local responsiveness to transform to a transnational organization focusing both, local responsiveness and global integration.[35]

2.3 Challenges when Implementing a Transnational Strategy

The major challenge has already become clear due to the explanation of the prior parts: coming from a strategy focusing a single dominant strategic demand, in the *ITT* case local responsiveness, the company needs to start developing global competitiveness and multinational flexibility simultaneously. Building these multiple strategic competencies is the primarily organizational challenge. It should allow the company to respond effectively to the new and complex demands of international business environments. *Bartlett* and *Beamish* describe the development of a transnational organization by using a framework based on a physiological model with the parts: organizational anatomy, physiology and psychology. Thus, management challenges can be described as follows:[36]

- **Structuring the Organizational Anatomy** (the formal structure of its assets, resources, and responsibilities): In a transnational organization, managers must develop supporting structures that supplement and counterbalance the embedded power of their dominant line managers. Having carefully defined the roles and responsibilities of geographic, functional, and product management, the next challenge is to ensure that particularly those without line authority have appropriate access to and influence in the management process.

- **Building the Organizational Physiology** (organization system's and decision processes): Management needs to develop the communication channels, through which the organization's decision-making process operates. By adapting the various administrative systems, communication channels, and informal relationships, information flows of management processes can be shaped. It is this flow of information that defines the organizational physiology. In such an integrated network configuration, as the transnational one, task

---

[35] Cf. Bartlett and Ghoshal (2002, pp. 12–13); Jones and Hill (2012, pp. 158–159); Peng (2008, pp. 295–305)
[36] Cf. Bartlett and Ghoshal (2002, pp. 286–289)

23

complexity and uncertainty are very high. Operating in such a multidimensional, interdependent system requires large volumes of information to be gathered, exchanged, and processed, so the role of formal information, planning, reporting and control systems is vital. But formal systems alone cannot support the huge information processing needs and companies are forced to look beyond their tradition tools and conventional systems.

- **Developing the Organization Psychology** (organization's culture and management mentality): The set of explicit or implicit corporate values and shared beliefs greatly influences the way its members act. Particularly when employees come from a variety of different national backgrounds, management cannot assume that all will share common values and relate to common norms. Furthermore, in an operating environment in which managers are separated by distance, language, and time barriers, shared management understanding is often much more powerful tool than formal structures and systems for coordinating diverse activities.

Following table summarizes these explanations.

Strategic Capability	Organizational Characteristics	Management Tasks
Global competitiveness	Dispersed and interdependent assets and resources	Legitimizing diverse perspectives and capabilities
Multinational flexibility	Differentiated and specialized subsidiary roles	Developing multiple and flexible coordination processes
Worldwide learning	Joint development and worldwide sharing of knowledge	Building shared vision and individual commitment

Table 2: Building and Managing the Transnational[37]

In the transnational company influence can be exercised by any nation on others and can start at any point, accumulating value as it goes and "circling" to reconcile cultural strength. What is important about transnationalism is that it follows circular cultural reconciliations, it combines the qualities of various cultures. Managers need to be aware of and deal with cultural differences as their daily business.[38]

[37] Cf. Bartlett and Ghoshal (2002, p. 77)
[38] Cf. Trompenaars and Hampden-Turner (2012, pp. 229–232)

Getting back to the case of *ITT*, despite its technological head start in researching digital signal processing, the company failed to integrate its substantial but dispersed technical resources and knowledge. The large systems houses balked at cooperating with one another and resisted accepting common standards. The biggest problem appeared when the company decided to take the new System 12 switch to the U.S-market, in response to the deregulatory moves of the early 1980s. In true *ITT* tradition, the U.S. group asserted its right to develop its own product and launched a major new R&D effort, despite appeals from the company's chief technological officer, who saw the effort as producing an ill-omened System 13. After years of effort and hundreds of millions of dollars in additional R&D costs, *ITT* acknowledged it was withdrawing from its home market because it had been unable to transfer and apply its leading-edge technology in a timely fashion. It was a failure that eventually led to further withdrawal from direct involvement in telecommunications worldwide.[39]

---

[39] Cf. Bartlett and Ghoshal (2002, p. 13); Viswanathan (1992, p. 71); Pollack (1986)

3. Joint Ventures in China

3.1 Introduction

China has the world second largest economy by nominal GDP.[40] There are several reasons for European companies to engage business in China, reaching from its attractive market to operational efficiencies/cost savings.[41] This part describes special challenges managers of a European companies face, when entering the Chinese market by a joint venture strategy. The focus is on companies that apply a global strategic approach.

3.2 International Joint Ventures (IJVs)

A joint venture involves an agreement by two or more companies to produce a product or service together. An IJV is among companies of different countries origin. In that case, the firm shares the profits, costs, and risks with a local or global partner and benefits from the partner's contacts and markets.[42] In an IJV, ownership is shared, typically by a MNE and a local partner, through agreed-upon proportions of equity. This strategy facilitates local contacts and familiarity with local operations. IJVs are a common strategy for corporate growth around the world. They also are a means to overcome trade barriers, achieve significant economies of scale for development of a strong competitive position, secure access to additional raw materials, acquire managerial and technological skills and spread the risk associated with operating in a foreign environment.[43] Not surprisingly, larger companies are more inclined to take a high-equity stake in an IJV to engage in global industries and be less vulnerable to the risk conditions in the host country. The IJV reduces the risks of expropriation and harassment by the host country.[44] Indeed, it may be the only means of entry into certain countries, such as Mexico and Japan, that stipulate proportions of local ownership and local participation.[45] For companies in emerging markets or developing economies, joint venture strategies provide opportunities to internationalize by gaining access to customers, supply networks, technology,

---

[40] Cf. International Monetary Fund (2017)
[41] Cf. Devonshire-Ellis (2011, pp. 1–2)
[42] Cf. Deresky (2016, p. 281); Nippa and Klossek (2004, p. 111)
[43] Cf. Zahra and Elhagrasey (1994)
[44] Cf. Pan and Li (2000)
[45] Cf. Deresky (2016, p. 263)

local brand image and knowledge, and natural resources. The local alliances also typically provide a learning curve for manufacturing, management skills, and technologies.[46] In recent years, the rate of IJV formation has continued to increase steadily, especially among emerging markets in Asia, Eastern Europe, and Latin America. These emerging markets account for about 70 percent of all IJV entries by MNEs. As companies deepen their business activities in low-cost centers and incorporate these endeavors into global value chains, their existing operating models may not be effective in emerging markets.[47] *Table 3* summarizes the advantages and disadvantages of IJVs.

Advantages	Disadvantages
- Lower capital requirement and risk - Avoiding "local-content" regulations and trade-barriers - Access to regional resources and knowledge - Building or changing of market barriers - Image advantages - Possible acquirement of funding programs or subsidies in foreign country - Fast market entry - Economies of Scale - Economies of Scope - Possibility of reduced competitiveness - Possibility of knowledge transfer	- High controlling and management resources needed - Potentially conflicting goals - Potential conflict in strategic alignment or profit distribution - Socio-cultural differences - Loss of influence- and control - Slower alignment of the JV to environmental changes - Laws and governmental regulations can influence the possibilities - Danger of stolen intellectual property and know-how

Table 3: Advantages and Disadvantages of IJVs[48]

3.3 Challenges for setting up International Strategic Alliances in China

IJVs are not just tools of convenience but are important – perhaps critical – means to compete in the global arena, to share in the immense costs involved and to share the risk burden. A strategic alliance, whether it may be an IJV or any other form, faces several challenges and is likely to fail. A study found that top management considered only 30 percent of strategic alliances as outright successes.[49] About 60 percent of IJVs fail, usually because of ineffective

[46] Cf. Deresky (2016, p. 263)
[47] Cf. Deresky (2016, p. 268); Giffi and Kambil (2009)
[48] Adopted from Perlitz and Schrank (2013, pp. 406–407); Kutschker and Schmid (2011, pp. 891–897)
[49] Cf. Cullen and Parboteeah (2014, p. 352)

managerial decisions regarding the type of IJV, its scope, duration, and administration as careless partner selection.[50] The further parts describe major challenges in detail.

3.3.1 Where to link the Value Chain

The objectives a firm hopes to achieve from an IJV determine where MNEs link in the value chain. In building alliances, each company must determine which of its value chain activities can be enhanced by having the relationships, thereby helping the firm achieve its strategic objectives. This is basically the first challenge managers face when planning an IJV. There are several options to link the value change:[51]

- Alliances that *combine the same value chain activities* often do so to gain efficient scales of operations, merge compatible talents, or share risks.
- In *operations alliances*, MNEs combine manufacturing or assembly activities to achieve a profitable volume of activities.
- *Marketing and sales alliances* allow companies to increase the scope and number of products sold and to share distribution systems.
- *Alliances linking upstream and downstream components of the value chain* can serve the objectives of low-cost supply or manufacturing.

3.3.2 Partner Selection

Most experts attribute the success or failure of strategic alliances to how well the partners get along. Especially early in the relationship, each party must believe that it has a good partner who can deliver on promises and be trusted.[52] The success of an IJV is essentially related to choosing the right partner. Thereby following challenges should be focused:[53]

- Conformable targets of both companies.
- Resources of the potential partner company.
- The partner helps the company to achieve strategic goals, which means the partner must have capabilities the company lacks and that it values.
- Trustworthiness between both companies

---

[50] Cf. Deresky (2016, p. 263)
[51] Cf. Cullen and Parboteeah (2014, pp. 352–355)
[52] Cullen and Parboteeah (2014, pp. 355–356)
[53] Cf. Holtbrügge and Puck (2008, p. 101); Jones and Hill (2012, pp. 218–219); Reden, Fischer, and Junkes (2004, pp. 95–98)

Many foreign executives prefer to engage with large, well-established Chinese partners. Yet that preference hasn't benefited JVs, typically because the parent companies didn't share the same strategic or commercial interests. Local, smaller companies that explicitly share the MNEs strategic goals should be considered. This opens the door to faster-growing, privately owned companies that bring a strong commercial mind-set and tangible business assets to JVs. As Chinese executives grow increasingly confident, many of these smaller players themselves hope to become national, regional, or even global players which is a drawback that foreign companies may encounter. That aspiration can make it difficult to agree on the scope of a partnership.[54] Following table summarizes critical factors for choosing the right partner.

Conformable Targets
- Conformability business targets between the potential corporation partner
Resources of the potential Corporation Partner
- Financial capabilities
- Location of the Enterprise
- Education and language skills of the Management and important employees
- Employee Contracts
- Availability of qualified or qualifiable workers
- Trustworthiness and reliability
- Position within the public hierarchy and economic relevance in the province
- Priority of the possible collaboration project
- Relationships (guanxi)
- Technology level of the products and condition of the plant(s)
Personal Trustworthiness between managerial directors
- Trust
- Combability of corporate cultures

Table 4: Critical factors for choosing the right partner corporation in China[55]

3.3.3 Choosing the Type of Joint Venture

There are two types of Joint Ventures in China, the Equity Joint Venture and the Contractual Joint Venture. An EJV is a joint venture between Chinese and foreign partners where profits and losses are distributed between the parties in proportion to their respective equity interests in the EJV. The foreign partner shall

---

[54] Cf. Bosshart, Luedi, and Wang (2010); Reuvid (2005, pp. 189–197); Reden et al. (2004, pp. 95–98); Nag (2011, pp. 203–204)
[55] Adopted from Holtbrügge and Puck (2008, p. 102)

hold more than 25% of the equity interest in the registered capital. An EJV is a new entity, partly owned by both sides, in which liability of the shareholders is limited to the assets they brought to the business. Thus, it enjoys limited liability, which does not extend to the parent companies. The CJV is a very flexible *Foreign-Investment Enterprise* where Chinese and foreign investor have more contractual freedom to structure the cooperation. It is basically a body of rules or network of contracts between two or more parties, often *called Non-Equity Forms of Cooperation*. Within a CJV, profits and losses are distributed between the parties in accordance with the specific provisions in the contract, not necessarily in proportion to their respective equity. It is mainly suitable for short-term projects. However, in practice EJVs are more common. Management needs to choose the right form of the IJV depending on its strategic goals and the expected length of the engagement.[56]

3.3.4 Public Regulations for Joint Ventures

The *Joint Ventures using Chinese and Foreign Investment* law from July 1st, 1979 and the *Equity Joint Venture law* of 1990 build the legal foundation of JVs in China. Additionally, the *Company Laws* come into account, as far as the earlier mentioned ones don't contain any topic specific regulations.[57] Joint Ventures are seen as foreign direct investments and underlie stronger regulations by the Chinese government as other market entry forms. For example, in industries as telecommunication, FDIs are prohibited completely, in the transport and logistics industry strictly limited. Since Chinas joining to the WTO, new opportunities for action raised, especially for IJVs. In technology and capital-intensive industries, especially in the construction and infrastructural sectors, CJVs are still preferred by the Chinese government. However, foreign majority investments are possible now, in previously restrictive treated industries.[58] The share of a foreign investor on an EJV should at least count 25%, hence the business counts as *Foreign Invested Enterprise*. This categorization is usually linked to benefits, e.g. tax exemptions. Applications on registration of a JV will usually be approved if the Chinese authorities can expect a modernization of the Chinese business, import

---

[56] Cf. Devonshire-Ellis (2011, pp. 4–39); Holtbrügge and Puck (2008, pp. 99–106); Shen (2008, pp. 64–70)
[57] Cf. Holtbrügge and Puck (2008, pp. 99–106); Devonshire-Ellis (2011, pp. 9–21)
[58] Cf. Nippa and Klossek (2004, p. 111)

substitutions, transfer of modern technology and management knowledge, increase in productivity, or the strengthening export of Chinese products. Managers need to inform themselves about the regulations and laws for the specific industry.[59]

3.3.5 Cultural Differences

Cultural differences can cause different understandings of the same thing. In international economic operations, it is difficult, if not impossible, to establish rules, such as those of the Olympic Games, that people from all cultures will abide by. When examining cultural differences, note should also be taken of the fact that China is moving towards a more open society. Increased interaction of Chinese people with westerners has prepared the ground for acceptance of western management concepts and practices. Following table is a list of key differences in the business context between Chinese and western cultures[60]

Chinese Culture	Western Culture
- Large power distance	- Small power distance
- Reverence to rank and power	- Equality among people
- Bureaucracy	- Authority of law
- Strong tendency of risk avoidance	- Strong tendency of risk traking
- Dominance of group interest and values	- Dominance of individualistic interest
	- Clarity in expression
- Doctrine of the mean and ambiguity	- Acceptance of change
- Resistance to change	- Pro-innovation
- Lack of original creativity	- Pursuit of objective being
- Pursuit of moral accomplishments	- Knowledge and skill learning
- Cultivation of personal virtue	- Recognition of material gains
- Despise material gains	- "Face" is unimportant
- "Face" is important	- Candor and rigidity
- Connotation and tolerance	

Table 5: Key differences between Chinese and western cultures[61]

Compared to German culture, huge cultural differences can be found in short-term vs. long-term orientation, individualism vs. collectivism, and power distance. Acknowledging cultural differences can be mentioned as one important success factor for establishing business in China. Managers are advised to prepare carefully and comprehensive.[62]

---

[59] Cf. Holtbrügge and Puck (2008, pp. 100–101)
[60] Cf. Yong and Baocheng (2005, pp. 158–160)
[61] Adopted from Yong and Baocheng (2005, p. 160)
[62] Cf. Holtbrügge and Puck (pp. 37–41); Hofstede and Bond (1988); Ehrhardt and Klossek (2004, pp. 51–66)

3.3.6 Negotiating the Agreement

Alliance contracts are the legal documents that bind partners together. The formal agreements, however, are never as important as the ability of managers to get along. In general, experts recommend that negotiation teams with technical and negotiation experience handle an alliance agreement. Cross-cultural negotiation skills are necessary.[63] Considerations should be done on following points:[64]

- What will the company's business scope be? Foreign invested enterprises, and indeed all domestic companies, must operate within their business scope – this is more critical than in most western countries.
- Is the business an "encouraged", "permitted", "restricted" or "prohibited" industry for foreign investment? This will determine whether you can in fact create a JV, and the incentives available or not.
- The texts of the company's *"Articles of Association"*. These will lead into consideration of issues like board structure, profits repatriation, trade unions, M&A, and liquidations.
- What should be the registered capital and total investment? This is a very important issue, and one will need to focus on it from an operational, not regulatory, point of view.
- For manufacturers: What proportion of production is for export, and what for domestic sales? A critical issue with major tax and operational proportion implication.
- Profit distributions and the sharing of responsibility for losses
- What taxes will the company need to pay?
- Where should the company be located?
- Are there any additional issues relating to the specific characteristics of JVs as: Who will be the leading party? Who will be in charge of sales or export sales? Is it necessary to allow one party to uniterally increase the registered capital, which would dilute the shares of the other party?
- What is the name of the new IJV company?

---

[63] Cf. Cullen and Parboteeah (2014, p. 362); Nippa and Klossek (2004, pp. 123–124)
[64] Cf. Devonshire-Ellis (2011, pp. 5–6); Cullen and Parboteeah (2014, p. 362); Bosshart et al. (2010)

3.3.7 Alliance Structure

An important factor is the alliance structure, which means reducing the company's risk of giving too much away to the partner. Following figure depicts the four safeguards against opportunism of cheating by alliance partners.[65]

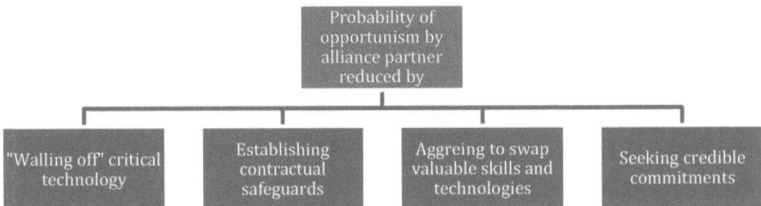

Figure 2: Structuring Alliances to Reduce Opportunism[66]

The concept of saving intellectual property is still new in China, and recourse to the legal system can be lengthy and inadequate. Managers need to be aware of this problem and make arrangements to guard the company's intellectual property.[67]

3.3.8 Organizational Design

IJVs require a separate organization to carry out the alliance's objectives. Thus, following points need to be considered regarding the organizational design:[68]

- **Decision-Making Control:** Operational decision-making and strategic decision-making need to be considered.

- **Management Structures:** To formalize the decision-making control partners must choose management structure that formally specifies the division of control responsibilities among partners. IJVs typically use five management control structures: dominant parent, shared management, split control, independent management, rotating management.[69]

Many characteristics of the alliance relationship influence the choice of a management structure.[70] Furthermore, structures can change as companies'

---

[65] Cf. Jones and Hill (2012, pp. 219–220)
[66] Adopted from Jones and Hill (2012, pp. 219–220)
[67] Cf. Bosshart et al. (2010); Desevadavy (2005, pp. 93–96)
[68] Cf. Cullen and Parboteeah (2014, pp. 363–364); Nag (2011, p. 204)
[69] Cf. Gray and Aimin (1992); Killing (2003);
[70] Cf. Cullen and Parboteeah (2014, p. 364)

needs or contributions to the alliance diverge.[71] Managers need to take following factors into account when designing a management structure for a joint venture:[72]

- Mature joint ventures move to independent structures as the IJV's management team gains expertise.
- Joint ventures in countries with a high degree of government intervention produce IJVs with local partner dominance. In China, this can be dependent on the industry, as mentioned (*Part 3.3.4).*
- Independent management structures are likely when the market is expanding, the venture does not require much capital, or the venture does not require much R&D input from its parents.

The ability to influence the course of a JV depends largely on the partners' ability to build trust-based relationships at the working level, the joint-venture board level, and even outside the joint venture, with the government, or other industry players. Successful multinationals map out critical stakeholders in and around the joint venture and assign relationships responsibilities at multiple levels of the organization.[73]

3.3.9 Managing the Alliance

When managing a joint venture with a Chinese partner, sensitivity to cultural differences is a key success factor. Many differences in management style are attributable to cultural differences, and managers need to make allowances for these in dealing with their partner. Beyond this, maximizing the benefits from an alliance seems to involve building trust and learning from partners. Managing an alliance successfully requires building interpersonal relationships between the firm's managers, or what is sometimes referred to as *relational capital.* The belief is that the resulting friendships help build trust and facilitate harmonious relations between the firms. Personal relationships also foster an informal management network between the firms. This network can then be used to help solve problems arising in more formal contexts. When entering an alliance, a company must take some measures to ensure that it learns from its alliance partner and puts that knowledge to good use within its own organization.[74] Multinational managers

---

[71] Cf. Bosshart et al. (2010)
[72] Cf. Cullen and Parboteeah (2014, pp. 364–365)
[73] Cf. Bosshart et al. (2010)
[74] Cf. Jones and Hill (2012, p. 220); Nippa and Klossek (2004, pp. 125–126)

need to consider several key factors to build and sustain commitment and trust in IJVs.[75] Studies have determined that a strong controlling the foreign partners activities can negatively affect trust within the partnership, which is highly critical for its success.[76] Despite trust, goodwill and strategic alignment, clear success factors can be found in maintaining a clear ownership structure, actively participate in daily operations and management, observing corporate culture differences, installing proper corporate governance procedures, avoiding unclear or risky legal situations, politically-sensitive plans, clipping local brands, sparking nationalist sentiment and prevent or manage negative publicity.[77] In summary, although IJVs often have a distinct advantage over internal new venturing or acquisitions, they also have certain drawbacks. When deciding whether to go it alone, acquire or cooperate with another company in a strategic alliance, managers need to assess carefully the pros and cons of the alternatives.[78]

---

[75] Cf. Cullen and Parboteeah (2014, pp. 367–368); Cullen, Johnson, and Sakano (2000); Bamford and Ernst (2002)
[76] Cf. Mohr (2002, pp. 214–216)
[77] Cf. Lee and Tan (2008, pp. 555–566)
[78] Cf. Jones and Hill (2012, p. 220)

4. References

Bamford, J., & Ernst, D. (2002). Measuring alliance performance. *McKinsey on Finance, 2*(3).

Bartlett, C. A., & Beamish, P. W. (2013). *Transnational Management: Text, Cases and Readings in Cross-Border Management* (7th ed.). Columbus: McGraw Hill Education.

Bartlett, C. A., & Ghoshal, S. (2002). *Managing Across Borders: The Transnational Solution* (2nd ed.). Boston: Harvard Business School Press.

Bosshart, S., Luedi, T., & Wang, E. (2010). Past Lessons for China's new joint ventures. *McKinsey Quarterly*. Retrieved from http://users.cla.umn.edu/~erm/data/sr486/govdocs/McKchina.pdf

Cullen, J. B., Johnson, J. L., & Sakano, T. (2000). Success through commitment and trust: The soft side of strategic alliance management. *Journal of World Business, 35*(3), 223–240. https://doi.org/10.1016/S1090-9516(00)00036-5

Cullen, J. B., & Parboteeah, K. P. (2014). *Multinational Management: A Strategic Approach* (6th ed.). Hampshire: Cengage Learning.

de Kluyver, C. A. (2010). *Fundamentals of Global Strategy: A Business Model Approach (Strategic Management Collection)* (1st ed.). New York: Business Expert Press.

Deresky, H. (2016). *International Management: Managing Across Borders and Cultures, Text and (9th Edition)* (9th). Essex: Pearson.

Desevadavy, F. (2005). Intellectual Property Rights in China. In J. Reuvid & L. Yong (Eds.), *Doing Business with China* (5th ed., pp. 93–96). London: GMB Pulishing Ltd.

Devonshire-Ellis, C. (Ed.). (2011). *Setting Up Joint Ventures in China (China Briefing)* (3rd ed. 2011): Springer.

Dudovskiy, J. (2017). Microsoft Value-Chain Analysis. Retrieved July 11, 2017, from Research Methodology: http://research-methodology.net/microsoft-value-chain-analysis-2-2/.

Ehrhardt, A., & Klossek, A. (2004). Die Relevanz kultureller Unterscheide in der deutsch-chinesischen Zusammenarbeit. In M. Nippa (Ed.), *Markterfolg in*

China. *Erfahrungsberichte und Rahmenbedingungen* (pp. 51–68). Heidelberg: Springer.

Galvin, P., Hubbard, G., & Rice, J. (2015). *Strategic Management: Thinking, Analysis, Action* (5th ed.). Melbourne: Pearson.

Giffi, C. A., & Kambil, A. (2009). Rethinking Emerging Market Strategies: From offshoring to strategic expansion. Retrieved June 18, 2017, from Deloitte: https://dupress.deloitte.com/dup-us-en/deloitte-review/issue-4/rethinking-emerging-market-strategies.html.

Gray, B., & Aimin, Y. (1992). A negotiations model of joint venture formation, structure, and performance: Implications for global management. In S. Prasad (Ed.), *Advances in International Comparative Management. V. 7* (pp. 41–75). JAI Press Inc.

Harzing, A.-W. (2000). An empirical analysis and extension of the Bartlett and Ghoshal typology of multinational companies. *Journal of international business studies : JIBS ; the journal of the Academy of International Business*.

Hofstede, G., & Bond, M. H. (1988). The Confucius connection: From cultural roots to economic growth. *Organizational dynamics, 16*(4), 5–21.

Hollensen, S. (2016). *Global Marketing (7th Edition)* (7th ed.). Harlow: Pearson.

Holtbrügge, D., & Puck, J. F. (2008). *Geschäftserfolg in China: Strategien für den größten Markt der Welt* (2nd ed.). Berlin: Springer.

International Monetary Fund. (2017). Report for Selected Countries and Subjects. Retrieved July 15, 2017, from IMF: http://www.imf.org/external/pubs/ft/weo/2017/01/weodata/weorept.aspx?sy=2015&ey=2022&scsm=1&ssd=1&sort=country&ds=%2C&br=1&pr1.x=71&pr1.y=6&c=924&s=NGDPD%2CNGDPDPC%2CPPPGDP%2CPPPPC&grp=0&a=.

Ireland, R. D., Hoskisson, R. E., & Hitt, M. A. (2006). *Understanding business strategy: Concepts and cases* (1st ed.). Mason: Thomson Higher Education.

ITT. (2017). ITT Geschichte. Retrieved July 14, 2017, from ITT: http://www.itt-deutschland.de/index.php/Ueber_ITT.html.

Jones, G. R., & Hill, W. L. C. (2012). *Essentials of Strategic Management: International Edition* (3rd ed.). Mason: Cengage Learning.

Killing, J. P. (2003). Understanding alliances: The role of task and organizational complexity. In F. J. Contractor & P. Lorange (Eds.), *International business and management series. Cooperative strategies and alliances* (2nd ed., pp. 241–245). Amsterdam: Pergamon.

Kutschker, M., & Schmid, S. (2011). *Internationales Management* (7th ed.). München: Oldenbourg.

Lee, S.-F., & Tan, M. (2008). Joint Ventures in China: Lessons to be Learned from Danone versus Wahaha. In D. Campbell (Ed.), *International Joint Ventures. The Comparative Law Yearbook of International Business* (pp. 544–593). Alphen aan den Rijn: Kluwer Law International.

Lombardo, J. (2017). Microsoft Corporation's Organizational Structure & Its Characteristics (An Analysis). Retrieved July 11, 2017, from Panmore Institute: http://panmore.com/microsoft-corporation-organizational-structure-characteristics-analysis.

Macharzina, K. (1993). Steuerung von Auslandsgesellschaften bei Internationalisierungsstrategien. In M. Haller, K. Bleichner, E. Brauchlin, H. J. Pleitner, R. Wunderer, & A. Zünd (Eds.), *... Wissenschaftliche Jahrestagung des Verbandes der Hochschullehrer für Betriebswirtschaft e.V: Vol. 54. Globalisierung der Wirtschaft. Einwirkungen auf die Betriebswirtschaftslehre* (pp. 77–109). Bern: Haupt.

McManus, J. T., White, D., & Botten, N. (2008). *Managing Global Business Strategies: A Twenty-First-Century Perspective. Chandos Business and Management*: Elsevier Science.

Mead, R., & Andrews, T. G. (2009). *International Management* (4th): Wiley-Blackwell.

Microsoft Corporation. (2016). Annual Report 2016. Retrieved June 18, 2017, from Microsoft Corporation: https://www.microsoft.com/investor/reports/ar16/index.html.

Mohr, A. T. (2002). *Erfolg deutsch-chinesischer Joint Ventures: Eine qualitative und quantitative* (1st ed.). Frankfurt am Main: Europäischer Verlag der Wissenschaften.

Morschett, D., Schramm-Klein, H., & Zentes, J. (2015). *Strategic International Management.: Text and Cases* (3rd ed.). Wiesbaden: Springer Gabler.

Nag, A. (2011). *Strategic Management: Analysis, Implementation, Control* (1st ed.). New Delhi: Vikas Publishing House.

Nippa, M., & Klossek, A. (2004). Erfolgsfaktoren internationaler Joint Venture in China: Ein praxisorientierter Review wissenschaftlicher Ergebnisse. In M. Nippa (Ed.), *Markterfolg in China. Erfahrungsberichte und Rahmenbedingungen* (pp. 107–136). Heidelberg: Springer.

Pan, Y., & Li, X. (2000). Joint venture formation of very large multinational firms. *Journal of international business studies, 31*(1), 179–189.

Peng, M. W. (2008). *Global Strategy* (2nd ed.). Mason: Cengage Learning.

Peng, M., & Meyer, K. (2016). *International Business* (2nd ed.). Hampshire: Cengage Learning.

Peng, M. W. (2016). *Global Business* (4th ed.). Boston: Cengage Learning.

Perlitz, M., & Schrank, R. (2013). *Internationales Management* (6th ed.). Konstanz: UTB GmbH.

Pollack, A. (1986). For Itt, an illusionary Promise. Retrieved July 15, 2017, from The New York Times: http://www.nytimes.com/1986/06/27/business/for-itt-an-illusory-promise.html?pagewanted=all.

PR Newswire. (2012). China's Wikipedia, Hudong.com to Help Bing in Search Model Revolution. Retrieved July 13, 2017, from PR Newswire: http://www.prnewswire.com/news-releases/chinas-wikipedia-hudongcom-to-help-bing-in-search-model-revolution-157190865.html.

Radebaugh, L. H., Daniels, J. D., & Sullivan, D. P. (2014). *International Business: Environments and Operations* (15th ed.). Essex: Pearson.

Reden, K., Fischer, U. A., & Junkes, J. (2004). Risikoanalyse und präventives Risikomanagement im Chinageschäft: Erfarhungen, Probleme und Erfolge beim Markteintritt. In M. Nippa (Ed.), *Markterfolg in China.*

Erfahrungsberichte und Rahmenbedingungen (pp. 87–105). Heidelberg: Springer.

Reuvid, J. (2005). Partner Selection and Negotiations. In J. Reuvid & L. Yong (Eds.), *Doing Business with China* (5th ed., pp. 189–197). London: GMB Pulishing Ltd.

Shen, W. W. (2008). China. In D. Campbell (Ed.), *International Joint Ventures. The Comparative Law Yearbook of International Business* (pp. 59–122). Alphen aan den Rijn: Kluwer Law International.

Trompenaars, A., & Hampden-Turner, C. (2012). *Riding the waves of culture: Understanding diversity in global business* (Rev. and updated 3rd ed. / Fons Trompenaars and Charles Hampden-Turner). London: Nicholas Brealey.

Virginia's Community Colleges. (2017). Microsoft Business Portfolio: Strategies for Reaching Global Markets. Retrieved July 11, 2017, from Virginia's Community Colleges: https://sites.google.com/a/email.vccs.edu/microsoft-business-portfolio/strategies-for-reaching-global-markets.

Viswanathan, T. (1992). *Telecommunication Switching Systems and Networks*. New Delhi: PHI Learning.

Waters, R. (2013). Steve Ballmer shakes up Microsoft structure in battle to compete. Retrieved July 13, 2017, from Financial Times: https://www.ft.com/content/0f60103a-ea3b-11e2-b2f4-00144feabdc0.

Wingfield, N. (2013). Microsoft Overhauls, the Apple Way. Retrieved June 04, 2017, from The New York Times: http://www.nytimes.com/2013/07/12/technology/microsoft-revamps-structure-and-management.html.

Yong, L., & Baocheng, L. (2005). Cultural Differences and Clashes in Communication. In J. Reuvid & L. Yong (Eds.), *Doing Business with China* (5th ed., pp. 158–166). London: GMB Pulishing Ltd.

Zahra, S., & Elhagrasey, G. (1994). Strategic management of international joint ventures. *European Management Journal, 12*(1), 83–93.